FAITH OVER FAILURE

REDEFINING FAILURE THROUGH THE LENS OF FAITH AND UNLOCKING YOUR GREATER POTENTIAL

COREY MANGUM

MEDIA & PUBLISHING

ISBN: 979-8-218-41393-4

About the Author

Who is Corey Mangum?

Corey Mangum is on a mission to develop leaders and motivate others to unlock their fullest potential, he has a passion for helping people see and live their greatest possible lives. He does this through Preaching, Coaching, Keynote Speaking & Published works.

Corey firmly believes that leadership initiatives should start at a young age, because of this belief, he developed and is the founder of Uncommon Youth International Inc., Mission "Ignite change in the lives of young people around the world". This non-profit organization was developed from his desire and passion to see the youth of our world reborn, experience a radical transformation, and to live a life that is "UNCOMMON" to society.

Corey is happily available for preaching, keynotes, workshops, panel discussions and other engagements.

Connect with Corey.

Email: coreylmangum@gmail.com

Youtube:
www.youtube.com/@coreymangum8425

Facebook:
https://www.facebook.com/Corey-
Mangum-109482508100840/

The M.E.S. (Motivation, Encouragement, and Success) Group on Facebook is an ideal source of inspiration from a community of people who are on their journey to pursue purpose and destiny. Link Below.

https://www.facebook.com/groups/13631
https://www.facebook.com/pg/UncommonY

THE IDEAL SPEAKER FOR YOUR NEXT EVENT!

Any organization that wants to develop their people to become "extraordinary," needs to hire Corey for a keynote and/or workshop training!

To Contact or Book Corey To Speak:

Coreymangum.com

Acknowledgments

To my "Good Thing" my wife, Mrs Alicia Mangum

I call her "Good Thing" because the Bible
declares in Proverbs 18:22(KJV)

"*He who* finds a wife finds a **good thing**,
And obtains favor from the Lord."

We have had our share of problems, yet God has continued to
bless us beyond belief. I am truly grateful for and to you Lady.

To my amazing children. Matejah, Izabel, Adrian, Justus,
Aryanna, Hadassah and Zion. I am beyond proud of
you all. You are my smile and my greatest dreams.

A large reason behind me writing this book is you. I want
you to retain these lessons and apply them to your lives
even after I am gone. The goal and task of a parent is to
elevate the next generation, ensuring they will succeed
beyond the successes of the previous, (their parents).

To my parents. First off, I apologize! After having kids
of my own, I GET IT!!! Y'all are the REAL MVPS!!

I've learned so many lessons from you and thank you for
all that you have given me in this life. You raised me in
the fear of the Lord and the mindset to always go BIG.

My sister Miss Aster D. Westbrook aka Danni.
You already know. Love you sis!

From Pasco WA to Yakima WA, to Arco ID, to Idaho Falls
ID, to Pocatello ID home all these places have taught me
so many great lessons about myself and life. Wow.

Contents

Introduction

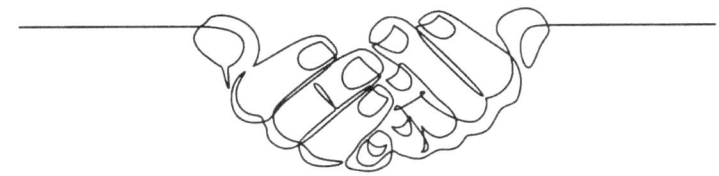

Hello Reader,

I can't tell you how excited and grateful I am, that you have decided to take this journey with me! Either you made the purchase of this book, or it was a gift or maybe you stole it. Either way, THANK YOU!

Success is a journey, you don't just get there overnight, there is work, effort, and more work that goes into reaching success. Your faith must align with your desires to see them come to life. I'm so glad that you've allowed me to take this journey with you.

I wrote this book as a devotional of sorts to help shift, reshape and or transform your mind. If you bring change to your mind, you do so to your life. Life generally occurs the way we perceive it. We have to see life from the lens of faith. Some people just need to wipe the dust of life and fear from their lens so they can see clearly. This book is that wipe you need.

This book was written in a devotional format, but you don't have to read it in that manner. There is a flow to the topics, yet, feel free to jump around from topic to topic. Break out your pen, pencil and or highlighter. Mark this bad boy up!

Get this book into the hands of your family members, friends, church members, coworkers and random strangers.

There are action items or questions at the end of each topic, which are designed to help you self assess, self discover and inspire your personal growth and transformation.

Let the journey begin!

Be Yourself

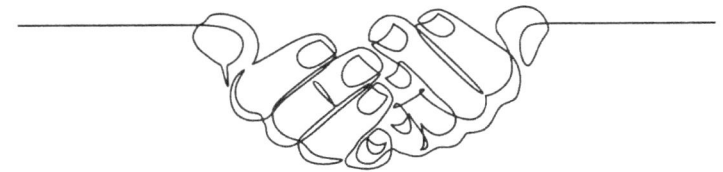

"I will praise thee; for I am fearfully and wonderfully made: marvelous are thy works; and that my soul knoweth right well".

Psalm 139:14 King James Version (KJV)

How can you be yourself if you don't know who you are? So my question to you is, who are you? How do you define who you are? What are you all about? What makes you come alive? What angers you? Your value becomes clear once you know who you are. We are all created with specific gifts, understanding or recognizing what your gift is will help provide the revelation of who you are.

I'm sure you've probably heard someone say "go find your gift". As if the gift is an external substance sitting on a shelf somewhere. We often speak of gifts like they are able to be purchased. Your gift is within you. **You are the gift.** You have something that needs to be manifested to the world. Those who do not deploy themselves or their gift will always chase after being the person other people say that they are. **Who are you?**

You are a one of a kind masterpiece. True personal success comes from a person knowing who they are, what they want and what they will give to the world. Your purpose in life will never be revealed or fulfilled as long as you are attempting to be someone or something you're not. This actually repels them. There are blessings that have been deployed to you, but they can't locate you when you are disguised as another individual. Your purpose, gifts and blessings are tied to your unique person.

We live in a competitive culture. Minus the participation trophies. Where people are constantly comparing themselves to others. It's bad when someone compares you to someone else, but what's worse is when you begin comparing yourself to other people. Recognizing differences is one thing, and in and of itself not bad, but to make comparisons as a means of validation is sick. This competitive mindset is very unhealthy and screams of insecurity. Example, someone uncomfortable with themselves, so they look to social media and/or television to compare their "likes", number of "follows", appearance, income etc., and attempt to duplicate that which they see in another person. Leaving them void, their true identity.

You can't legally give away what's not yours to give. So many people discard their identity, pick up another and attempt to display or give away the counterfeit version of themselves to the world with the expectation of being happy or fulfilled. At some point the true you will come to the surface.

It takes a tremendous amount of pressure to suppress who you are and maintain a false identity. This has to be one of the worst types of bondage. Suicide, addiction, abuse and more, can all be linked to this issue. **STOP TRYING TO BE SOMEONE YOU'RE NOT**. You can add years to your life and experience so much more peace if you just be yourself.

What you don't see is the struggle it took for most of those stars to get where they are and many of them face ugly struggles now. You only see the smiles and fun times, they don't show you the broken hearts, loneliness, depression, addiction, late nights, grind and HARD WORK that they battle every single day. Some of these folks are also wearing masks. So you're comparing yourself to, disguising yourself as and trying to duplicate a person or people who aren't even being their true self or know who they truly are? Not a good place to be in. Limited editions are always more valuable than carbon copies and duplicates. The rarer the object, the higher the demand and value. Diamond versus Cubic zirconia. From the standpoint of value cubic zirconia is worth next to nothing. The real you is priceless while the duplicate version can't provide anything of true value.

I suggest you take some time alone to learn, you. Learn who you are and what you are about. I'm going to go out on a limb and say you may not know who you truly are but are interested in meeting your true self. You're not the only one. Countless people have been living in that same place.

Get in a quiet place and ask yourself the following questions to help jumpstart a conversation with yourself to better understand who you are. Tell you about you.

1. How do you define who you are?

2. What are you all about? What drives you?

3. What makes you come alive or brings you joy?

4. What angers you?

5. What are you naturally good at?

6. What do you like most about yourself? (not physical)

7. What do you dislike about yourself? (not physical)

8. What is your biggest struggle?

9. What is your number one fear?

10. What obstacles have you overcome to get to where you currently are in life?

IT!

In this book and many motivational speeches, you will often come across the word "IT". But no one explains what it is. Do you have an "it"? Have you discovered your "it"? Can you get an "it"? Who all has an "it"? It is that thing, that thing that makes your heartbeat a little faster. That thing that you've envisioned. That thing your dream about and imagine that you have **it**. That thing that you were born or created to do. That thing that keeps you up late at night. That thing that makes you want to quit your job to chase after "**it**". "**It!**" Such a powerful thing. "**It.**" It needs you, "**it**" can't survive without you, "**it**" won't come into fruition without you. It has no ability to impact your life nor generations to come if you don't help "**it**".

"**It**", Is your education, your wonderful idea, your new business innovation, your promotion, new job, new relationship, your desired weight loss/muscle gain/body transformation. "**It**", is whatever you are working towards and desire to see come to pass in your life. We all have a dream and a desire for better, it's up to us to make **it** a reality. No one can do it for us.

GO FOR "IT"!

Notes for
Faith over Failure

Change Your Life

"Change is inevitable. No matter the action you take, change will come. The power is yours to direct change towards the direction you desire. Positive or negative."

Corey Mangum

You say you want to see change in your life, right? I believe you. Others believe in you. The only problem is, you don't believe you. If you did, you would do the things required for change to occur. The desire has to match the level of potential actions and participation in which you must take. Does your level of desired change match the level of sacrifice it takes to make that change happen? Are you willing or ready to get up off the couch, exercise and be committed to being uncomfortable to get the health/life that you desire?

When we set our affections on things above, we gain the byproducts of the affections above, meaning, we should go to the gym, exercise and eat healthy to sustain our bodies and a good quality of life. A nice body while great to have, look at and show off, is just the byproduct of your desire and actions aligned.

When your desires and actions collide it causes a chain reaction of change, growth and ultimately success. You have to empower yourself to make a move in the direction you desire.

I know there are so many things standing in the way. Your work/school schedule, your kids' sports, your favorite show is getting SO good, you get bored easily and have to snack to keep yourself entertained. I get it. You have an excuse, just like everyone else. Congratulations, you're just like everyone else, you have excuses, please don't be like everyone else and continue to live in your excuses, but be a trailblazer in a jungle somewhere and pull out your machete of desire and victory and hack your way through those excuses right to the destination of change.

Change to a certain extent is inevitable. It's sad to see how people age physically, but never mentally, emotionally or spiritually mature. Change happens, you can't stop it. Change and time are besties; they operate on the same accord. Just as the seasons change with time, and we see the evidence thereof, in the changing of the leaves, grass turns brown or green, the temperature shifts and the sun sets or rises sooner. Just like nature experiences change, so will you. The unique thing about mankind and change is that you can play a major part in your personal change or, you can sit back and just let it happen to you. Why wouldn't you give your input? Why would you let nature dictate to you how you will get along?

Each action has a reaction. Sit on the couch, eat all the junk food/ fast food, don't read, study or work at personal growth, skip leg day. Lol whatever it is now, and there is a reaction or change associated. Or you can do the opposite and find another set of results. The choice is yours. No one can stop you but you, likewise no one can do it for you except you.

What are you waiting for? Do you need the clouds to part, the earth to shake or an audible voice to speak to you and tell you to get up? Well it's happening right now, the words you're reading are the clouds parting, earthquake and the life altering voice you've been waiting for. Now let's go!

Are you an active participant in your life's changes? If yes, how so? If not, why not?

Has your participation been positive or negative?

List 3 positives

1. _____

2. _____

3. _____

List 3 negatives

1. _____

2. _____

3. _____

What can you do TODAY that can help you move forward with positive change?

What are you going to do TOMORROW?

Purpose

*To every thing there is a season, and a time
to every purpose under the heaven:*

Ecclesiastes 3:1 KJV

*The LORD has made everything for its purpose,
even the wicked for the day of trouble.*

Ecclesiastes 3:1 ESV

I often have conversations with people about how to grow in life and about being successful. After listening to a person talk about life for a moment, it becomes apparent whether the individual has or has not discovered their purpose.

Purpose
What is purpose?

I was in a business mastermind group listening to a presenter who delivered a Q&A presentation on the topic.

The presentation wasn't bad at all, in fact she did a great job engaging the audience and answering questions. There was a question asked about functioning in your purpose, she said "well your purpose changes depending on the day, and or time of day etc.." When I heard that, I asked myself a question. "Self, she said that purpose is constantly changing and if other people believe that or are teaching that, could that be the reason why so many folks are confused about purpose?"

What do you think? Is purpose fluid, always changing or shifting based upon environment or circumstances?

I think not.

Purpose is constant, consistent, and unmoved. Purpose is the original intent or reason for something's existence or creation. A carpenter's hammer, for example, has the purpose of driving nails. Its purpose does not change when it is used for something else or taken into a strange environment. Its purpose remains intact. The reason for its creation doesn't change because the season or circumstances change. The vision of the creator was not altered.

Purpose does not change due to location or date. Assignments, missions, objectives and goals may change based upon these factors yet your purpose remains. Assignments, missions, objectives and goals are all dictated upon environments and timeframes, because they lead to you fulfilling your purpose there in that place.

I want to affirm the fact that you were created with a specific thought in mind. Your creator has a purpose for you. Don't allow circumstantial noise, situations, people, environments or anything else to drown out the revelation that you have a purpose and it was given to you by your creator before you were born.

Jeremiah 29:11

The Creator hasn't changed His mind about you or your purpose on the Earth. He knew about all of your shortcomings and excuses when He thought His best thoughts about you and gave you the Life altering, world changing, purpose you've had from your very beginning. Before your parents even thought about you. That's heavy.

Secret

You're just as able now as you were back then. Just as good, worthy and acceptable. You just have to function within it.

Jeremiah 1:5

Before you were born God formed you and knew exactly what He was doing and what the world needed from you (what your purpose was to be). For Jeremiah, specifically, his purpose was to prophecy and fulfill the office of the prophet.

Three key words to focus on in Jeremiah 1:5

1. Sanctified—Set apart or separated from the pack
2. Ordained—Stamp of approval
3. Prophet—Title, office or function (unique job)

God has done the same thing concerning you. Maybe you're not a prophet or preacher. Think on the terms of being set apart, stamped with approval and then given an office that you function in. He has ordained you to be a teacher, business person, social/cultural influence, maybe something in the fields of justice or law, administration or maybe even music. All I know is that you were created on purpose, with a purpose and that's to fulfill a purpose.

What is it that you do that comes natural? Where do you excel where others struggle? When you are in your purpose you are in your vein or flow. It's like the current of the river, a natural flow. You never see a river fighting itself, you know, a portion of the water trying to flow against the rest. It's all in a synchronized flow. This is how purpose looks. Not to say that everyday will be the brightest day nor that you will never face adversity but when you are in your flow you know.

What is your purpose? (why you were created)

How are you executing your purpose?

What is it that you do that comes natural?

Where do you excel where others struggle?

How or where can you begin to apply your strengths in your personal life to make a difference?

"Plan your steps and find success.

Success doesn't come by chance."

- Corey Mangum

Vision

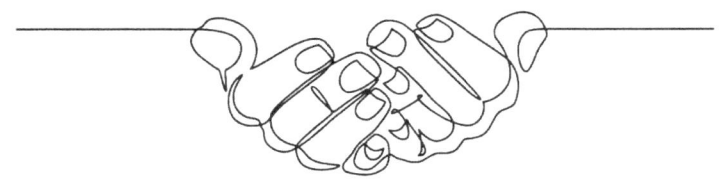

"Where there is no vision, the people perish:
but he that keepeth the law, happy is he."

Proverbs 29:18 King James Version (KJV)

Vision is the launch pad of success. Before you can set out to accomplish anything, it must first start in your mind. If you can see it, it's possible. A good way to describe vision is in the climber preparing to ascend a mountain but before any action takes place, he or she is able to see them themselves at the summit. So in other words the destination or the final product.

Do you have a vision for your life? In addition, do you have a vision for your family, business, ministry, or career? Vision is the prerequisite to success in every aspect and area of life. Where one lacks vision, they meet demise. Countless people are successful at aimlessness. Meaning they have little to no direction for their life trajectory, just wandering through life without knowing and in some cases caring where they are going. Drifters, tossed to and fro by the waves of life.

What do you want in life? Where do you want to go in life? What does it look like? What does a maximized life look like to you?

The lack of vision opens the door to destruction and your inevitable perish. Marriages that lack vision are more likely to end in divorce. We've all seen or heard of the lottery winners who have no vision or idea of what to do with the large sum of money, blow their winnings and end up worse than they were before they won. Everyone wants good things and wants to live the "good life" but that which they desire they will not have because you can not have what you can not see in your mind first.

Every invention we see started as a vision. Every artist's beautiful masterpieces first existed as a vision in their mind's eye, they had an idea of what the end product would be, they worked to make that vision come to life and we behold that product in amazement. You have that same ability, you just have to unlock it with the power of vision. If you can see, believe, and put in the work, that vision can begin to breathe and live.

Get a vision
Take time alone, close your eyes and envision what you want in life. Be as detailed as possible.

Now write that down. (there is space in the back of the book)

What do I want my life to look like? In.

5 years:

10 years:

20 years:

Where do you want to go in life?

What does a maximized life look like to you?

Describe your vision of these areas of life:

Relationship with God—

Marriage—

Family—

Career—

Finances—

Faith

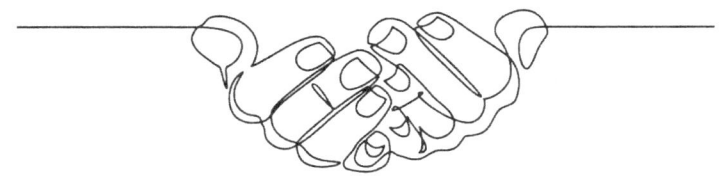

"Now faith is the substance of things hoped for, the evidence of things not seen."
Hebrews 11 King James Version (KJV)

Faith. Faith is such an amazing thing. Faith is one of the most difficult things to explain or even understand. Faith is the genetic makeup of everything you hope for and without it nothing is possible, yet with faith **ALL** things, everything, anything is **possible.**

Faith is the key ingredient to the recipe of your destiny and Success.

Faith is the driving force behind your life's vision.

On the topic of faith: When God gives you a vision, He is showing you what He sees as potential. When you have the ability to see what God sees, you can speak what God Speaks and bring change like He brings change. Faith is you acting out or towards what you see. A person who aspires to become a doctor, works toward the end goal, that work is them going to school, training and anything else required. They have no first hand experience in the steps needed to accomplish their aspiration yet they take each step as an act of faith. The work applied is the substance of their desire.

People without vision wander because they lack direction, expectation or sense of purpose. Faith/expectation is future based, no one expects for the past because it's gone and cannot be changed. Expectation reaches forward to grip the hand of what is to come. Then by faith your efforts pave a road for that expected end to come to you.

Faith is the needed fuel for the vehicle which carries you to your destination.

Where is your faith?

When the level of your faith is determined by your own abilities or lack thereof, you limit your power and possibilities to succeed, as well God's access to operate on your behalf. Several times in the Bible we see Jesus tell someone "your faith has made you whole". We must understand the level of faith dictates our level of altitude.

You can only go as far as your faith will take you.

Without faith you stagnate, you lack creativity, and vision for the future. Faith is a present to future thing. Faith does not live in your past, it can only exist and dwell in your present and future. We can reach back into our past and see how far faith has brought us. We learn lessons from the past, but faith will not take us back into the past. **Faith always moves forward.**

Many people look at themselves and focus on their weaknesses, shortcomings, mistakes and past failures then use them as excuses as to why they can't achieve. Your weakness doesn't make things impossible, faith makes what seems impossible, possible. "All things are possible to him that believe". (Mark 9:23 kjv). You have to see yourself doing the impossible before it becomes possible (vision).

How do you define faith?

Faith can be seen in the actions of a farmer. When a farmer goes out to sow seed, he or she does so as the evidence of the harvest which they hope for, expect, but do not see. Many things in your life will not come to pass due to a lack of faith in what you do not see. You have to get to the place in faith that you tell yourself "even though I don't see it", meaning you will begin to sow the seeds of action toward the fruition of your vision and the things that you hope for. **This is how you bring your faith to life!** Remember "faith without works is dead". James 2:17. Faith is an action word, it requires action coupled with belief and expectation of what you can't see.

What are your future expectations?

Family

Finances

Career

Education

Spiritual

Fear Not

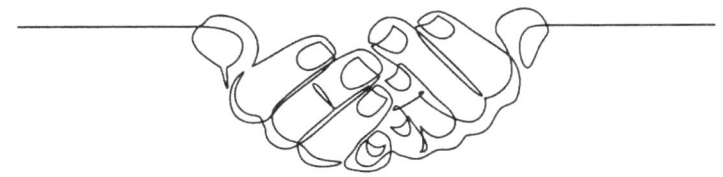

"For God hath not given us the spirit of fear; but of power, and of love, and of a sound mind."

2 Timothy 1:7 KJV

Fear is an emotion every human being possesses as a source of protection or defense. Fear in and of itself isn't necessarily a bad thing, as long as it's held in its proper perspective. Fear is designed to help one protect themselves from legitimate harm or threats. Fear becomes unhealthy when manipulated. Perceiving most things seen and unseen as threatening is the manipulation of fear. We have been conditioned to live in a constant state of fear (unhealthy fear). Fear conditioning is a behavioral paradigm in which organisms learn to predict aversive events. This is when common events or objects are coupled with negative response which, when repeated, trains the brain to think in the context or conditions of fear. In other words you have dreams, ambitions and ideas of greatness yet your brain is predicting or showing you negative outcomes, as a result of the stimuli in which you have been surrounded.

Healthy fear is nothing more than reverence of respect for what may lie ahead. Walking forward alert to what may lie ahead or behind. We respect and have a "fear" of electricity and fire, because if we don't the outcome can spell certain demise. It is when we take that same outcome and apply it to every decision we make or do not make. Applying fear in this manner leads to a stagnant existence.

A certain amount of fear can be and is healthy, as I said it's a protective or defensive mechanism. Imagine a child with fear of harm playing with fire, knives, broken glass or a loaded gun. The child or someone nearby is in danger of harm. This is where fear can be helpful to inspire wisdom. Due to lack of life experience the child lacks the cognizance of possible dangers.

Fear if left unchecked and allowed to over act in one's mind can oftentimes cause paralysis of progress in their life, leaving them seated in firm self doubt. This is the birthplace of self inferiority "God has not given us the spirit of fear, but rather a spirit of power, love and a sound mind or self-control."(2 Timothy 1:7). When you live in a place of perpetual fear you are no longer in control of yourself. Fear becomes your master. Being controlled by fear sets limits to your abilities in life, it tells you where you can and can't go, what you can and can't do and how far you can go. **IT'S TIME TO TAKE YOUR POWER BACK FROM FEAR!**

Fear has fooled you. Fear has fooled countless people with lies of failure, defeat and shame. Those individuals cease to resist and submit to the authority of fear, in full surrender. The authority of fear is a lie. **FEAR HAS NO AUTHORITY OVER YOU.**

IT'S TIME TO TAKE YOUR POWER BACK!

How can we say we love ourselves when we live as we have succumbed to fear. Love is that thing that encourages us to do, give and be our best. Love causes us to be kind, patient, peaceful and joyful. Love provides freedom, where fear brings captivity and hatred. The more we love the less fear can take root in our lives. **IT'S TIME TO TAKE YOUR POWER BACK!**

When you dismiss fear, the "sound mind" tells you that you are safe, secure and able to live your fullest life. The sound mind relays the message that you are in control and that you have nothing to fear. This is the truth that fear does not want you to know. Woodrow Wilson once said "fear God and you need not fear anyone else". In this term, the word "fear" is used in the idea of respect and or honor. Don't allow unhealthy fear to move you out of the place of respect and honor, into that of shame and degradation. **IT'S TIME TO TAKE YOUR POWER BACK!**

There are 3 main areas where fear takes up residents in one's mind.

1. What might happen

2. What others might say

3. What if I'm not good/I might fail

Fear of what might happen works against your faith and the possibilities of success.

Fear of what others might say is you surrendering to the opinions of others.

Fear of failure or not being good enough is the expectation of lack.

DECLARATION: (recite this declaration for the next 30 days)

> **I declare that I take my power back. I love
> myself and fear does not control me. I
> am free and my mind is at peace.**

Where (areas of life) have you fought fear?

Have you been paralyzed by fear?

What actions can you take to show fear that you're in control?

THE POWER IS YOURS!

Its time to break the chains of oppression from your thinking

Corey Mangum

Existing in bandage is not living.

Wins and Losses

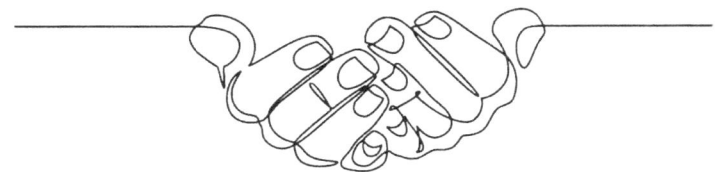

As long as you're alive wins and losses will occur. We've all heard the saying "you win some, you lose some". This phrase is usually followed by an unapologetic shrug of the shoulders from the person reciting it, in a half hearted attempt to console or offer solace.

None of us want to put a check mark in the losses column, we would prefer to go through life undefeated. However this is unrealistic, "rain falls on the just as the unjust" (Matthew 5:45) During the times of rain or loss we can easily get lost in the gloom but remember without rain we go into drought, where drought goes famine follows, then death, we need rain.

We've been trained to view wins and losses in the wrong way. Winning feels great and it's true losing hurts, yet I want to help you retrain your brain. For the longest time we have treated victories as ego boosts and every loss or defeat as a point of shame, a deflating force piercing the Hot Air balloon of our success, leaving us to plummet in fear filled doubt into destruction of self worth.

Our victories or wins in life are helpful in promoting self worth, which is good, but should also serve as a reminder that you can overcome any obstacle set before you. Victories are testimonies that cry out to your future the knowledge that you are a powerful person able to achieve greatness. Without an obstacle or opponent there can be no victory.

Losses should be regarded as training tools or strength builders. Just like weights in the gym. Losses help us exercise the muscles of our character. Are you a winner or a loser? Are you weak or are you strong? The answer is defined by how you respond to losses. When you go through hard times or something trouncing, don't let it destroy you, or your faith, use it as training or preparation for future battles and victories. Ultimately we should extract life lessons for our perfection from our losses. You were made to win, you were created in the image of a winner. (Genesis 1:26 & 27) The one that created you has never lost, and will never be defeated. Decide now, that you are a WINNER!

The struggle is real but so is the victory on the other side of the battle. Don't be fooled by difficulty, be encouraged by it. The more losses the stronger you become, if you could begin to see yourself from this lens you would see how jacked, ripped and strong you actually are. You look like a bodybuilder. Think about the last huge loss or battle you overcame. If you can survive that, you can make it through anything. YOU ARE A WINNER! Now go out and win!

"Strength and growth come only through continuous effort and struggle."

Napoleon Hill

What was the last big defeat you came up against?

How did you get through it?

What did you learn from it?

List 7 of your most memorable victories?

1. _____

2. _____

3. _____

4. _____

5. _____

6. _____

7. _____

What have your victories taught you?

Take the Risk

The greatest risk in life is to avoid them, where there is no risk there can be now reward.

Corey Mangum

Everything you set out to do or even imagine doing carries a certain amount of risk. To be successful at anything requires you to leave the comfort of the familiar and step into uncertain territory. For some, they tiptoe into risk, others launch themselves into it, and some fall somewhere in between. Well, wherever you are on the "risk taking spectrum" **GET UP** and **GO FOR IT!**

Now when talking about risk, we have to use wisdom. This is why having a vision and planning are so crucial. These absolutely do not void risk from the equation, however when you have a vision and create a plan to bring it to fruition, you can more easily assess the risks associated with every step required to reach the goal.

The people you look up to and admire with such high regard, because of the things that they've accomplished, took great risks to get to the place in life that they are. You're no exception. To get to the next level in life you're going to have to take some risks. Accept that and don't back down.

Jumping head first from an airplane naked with no parachute is not a risk. It's stupidity and a death wish. Silly I know. But this is what so many people think of, when you mention taking risks towards achievement.

Now imagine someone actually jumping from an airplane naked, without a parachute and they hit the ground. What will people say or think? How big will the news report be? Imagine the questions and comments.

Why did he do it?

Why naked?

Why didn't friends or family stop them or know what was going on?

Must have had some mental condition...

Probably came from a hard life...

Too much pressure...

I know that person, I always said he/she was crazy.

One of the biggest reasons many people refuse to step out in faith and take the risk, is they fall into the crushing, depressive and oppressive questions, opinions and comments of others. Most people's opinion about the risks you take are based upon their fears. People will always try to find a way to project their inabilities on you. Most of them have never even attempted to do what you are dreaming of and would never take the chance to make it happen.

Growing up my parents started a barbecue restaurant in the small town of Arco, Idaho. This town's population was one thousand people, and there were five Black people in town. My dad, mom, sister, brother and me. So many people questioned and doubted my dad in the process of starting his business and had question upon question about how he would make it work, especially since there were no black people to support him. Not to mention he was taking early retirement from a great paying government job. So he must have seemed crazy. I remember my dad telling me that his vision was to have people from all walks of life and from all over coming to eat in little ole Arco Idaho. His risk paid off. We have been in business for over 26 years, and have had people from all over the world dine with us. This would have never occurred had he not stepped out and took the risk.

Most times when someone is hyper critical towards the risks of others it's because they are jealous that they lack the vision or courage to leave their comfort zone and take a chance to be great. FORGET what other people have to say, they're going to talk about you either way, whether to take the risk or not. Either they'll say I can't believe he or she is going to do that, it is so risky or they'll say, he or she is too scared to take that risk, it is too much for them. Either way they're going to have something to say. So you might as well just, **TAKE THE RISK!**

Life is Short

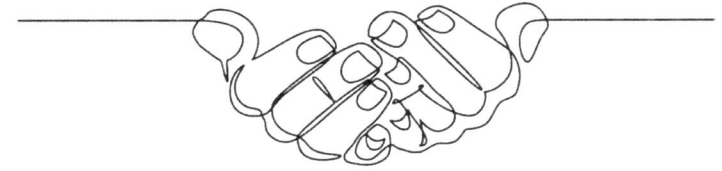

"Whereas ye know not what shall be on the morrow. For what is your life? It is even a vapour, that appeareth for a little time, and then vanisheth away".

James 4:14 (KJV)

2013, the fourth of July. Independence Day. My younger brother died. He drowned in the Snake River in Idaho Falls, Idaho. Just before the fireworks were ignited. Each burst of light and bright color was amazing as we watched the show, yet totally unaware of what was to come. The local sheriffs called and asked my parents if they had seen or heard from my brother. Around 11:00 pm, I received a panicked call from my mom wondering if I knew where my brother was. Then she said the most heart wrenching thing that I had heard to that point in my life, "the police think he fell into the river, and no one saw him come out".

In a rush, I jumped out of bed, got dressed and went to every place I had known him to hang out at. With no luck

I headed to my parents house to check in and see if they had received any updates.

The feeling in the house was completely still. It was as if nothing, not even the clock had permission to move, as time stood still, and we waited in anticipation for him to call, walk through the door, or receive news of some kind, hopefully positive. There was such heaviness in the room that words can't explain. We prayed and barely talked, more like whispering, then prayed some more, believing for the best.

2:00am comes with an uncertain knock at the door. Dad opens the door and it's the Sheriff. As he walked in you could see the weight of the news on his face and countenance. He addressed my mom, sitting on the couch, at the same time fighting with his own emotions and said: "We've found him". After hearing those words there was a pause. Time stood still and in that moment the earth paused its rotation. Until my mom dropped to the ground and released a loud cry of torment, jarring, soulful, excruciating pain that words can't fully explain, but revived time and reality which was held in suspense.

My brother was 27 years old when he lost his life. That was way too soon.

Life is short. It's time to go for it. I don't know what it is that you are dreaming of, have a heart for or are currently working on but I have to say it again, **LIFE IS SHORT. IT'S TIME TO GO FOR IT.**

I don't say that in a ra-ra cheerleader, empty kind of way, I say that with all sincerity and heartfelt emotion. I mean you only get one shot at this life thing and it's short. S get up, get out and live life. Turn off the TV, get off the couch and LIVE. Go on that dream vacation. Do something with or for your spouse that makes them smile. Play catch with your son, fetch with the dog, dress up with your daughters. Something, just don't sleep your life away. Every hour, minute and second that goes by will NEVER return. Life is short and you never know when your time is up.

Imagine living your entire life and at the time of your passing you're burdened with the guilt of incomplete desires, hope and expectation that were never given the chance to live. You have to understand that life and time are precious and once they are gone, they don't come back. Treat every project, relationship and event like it's your last, it actually is. You can't relive first impressions. Everything we do is a first and last impression as time can not be reversed.

When you start looking at life from the lens of life being short, you make every present opportunity count. Life is a vapor that appears then disappears just as fast as it appeared. Make your life count. **LIFE IS SHORT.**

No One Can Do *It* For You

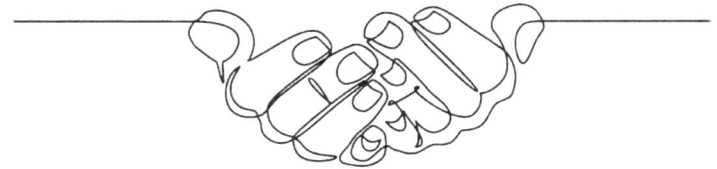

That dream you have, the goals you've set, the vision that you've seen, the big life changing idea or business plan. No one can bring that thing to life, except you.

Many times in life we come across people or things that look good or seem like "if i just had that thing or that person, it would make the dream a reality or make life easier". As you say that your accomplishment is locked up in something or someone. So you're looking at external factors. Well can I just tell you that, it's not true. Your dream, vision, plans and ideas are waiting on you.

Parents, spouse, friends, co-workers, siblings. No one can make it happen for you. You are the only one who has what it takes to make it happen. The reason it hasn't is lack of preparation. Of course we will find people to help with the work but the initiation of success is all on you. We have to prepare for success and not rely on something or someone else to make it happen. Nothing and no one you find will make success happen for you.

If you really embrace the idea that it all falls on you, you can then determine or assess the things needed to make it happen. You have to take control. You have been given the authority to make things happen without depending on anyone else.

Relationships are or can be difficult to manage especially during times of frustration and discomfort. It is always easier to point fingers and place blame on the other person in the relationship. This releases you from any and all levels of responsibility to fix the issues at hand and it's the same thing when it comes to focusing on success and personal growth.

Take responsibility
No matter what's going on in your life, you have to be responsible for yourself and where you are. Take control, take charge.

You have to take ownership of every situation. When you place responsibility on another person it takes away your control and leaves you at the mercy of another. In every area of life you have to own where you are in life, once you do that you can freely and quickly move forward. Things may not be your fault but victims can never be victors until they are no longer victims. I'm not suggesting that you shift blame of guilt from the guilty party to yourself. But, **DO NOT RELY ON THE GUILTY TO FIX THE ISSUE.** You take control for yourself and begin to move forward.

Your success requires your personal touch, it craves your DNA, and without you showing up to make it happen, it will remain incomplete or hidden from reality. No one can do it for you. Whatever you lack, it's your responsibility to gain it. Education, books, experience, or a specific product, whatever it is it's on you. If you dodge responsibility you dodge the power to make a difference in your own world.

Mother Tersea took responsibility for the poor, sick and needy. She wasn't at fault, nor the cause of their destitute situation but she took ownership of those particular issues and was able to make a massive difference in the world, and in her death her name still carries weight.

Dr. Martin Luther King Jr. took responsibility for racial injustice and inequality. Not his fault but his proactive and head-on approach showed the opposition that change was needed and many changes happened based upon those activities. He didn't wait on the opposing side to own up to their guilt and fix the issues, he and those that accompanied him firmly took action and did so in the face of possible death and certain ridicule.

Michael Jordan took responsibility for the city of Chicago, the Bulls team and his own personal basketball game/level of play. Now he is regarded as one of, if not the greatest basketball player of all time.

These are just 3 examples of the power of taking ownership and responsibility for your success. Not only will it help your life but can affect others and future generations as well. You may work alone, or as part of a team, either way you must take ownership of the mission at hand. No one can do it for you.

Stop looking for handouts.

Stop making it someone else's issue.

Stop passing the buck.

Stop dodging the work.

Stop sitting on the couch waiting for someone else to do it for you.

Your attention and hands are required.

There are so many obstacles and temptations we face in life which all but take the very life from our bodies. So difficult, heart wrenching and sometimes shameful. The trials you face, no one can overcome them for you. You have to find the power within and fight back until you see victory.

Read—John 16:33(KJV) "I have told you these things, so that in me you may have peace. In this world you will have trouble. But take heart! I have overcome the world."

Jesus Himself had to take ownership of the mission set before Him, the fulfillment was His responsibility. Without Him, redemption would have never happened. He tried to find another way because of the cost and pain. But it was certainly worth it. Read Matthew 26:39 in the Bible to see what I mean.

No matter the area of life, no one can achieve fulfillment or success for you. You have to have some skin in the game. You're looking for a surrogate, someone to carry it, endure the pain, discomfort and scars, whilst you get the reward of their labor. There is no such thing in the arena of success. **NO ONE CAN DO IT FOR YOU**. Get up and make it happen.

Notes for
Faith over Failure

"You can't live in your destined future, until you've left your past."

Corey Mangum

Victim or Victor?

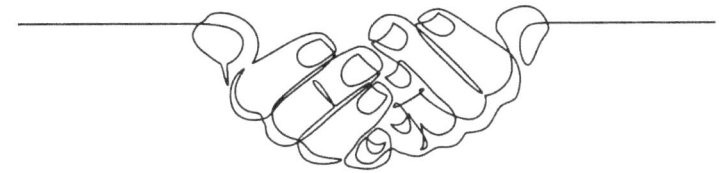

Before we get started let's make this declaration. **I AM NOT A VICTIM!**

After reading this I hope this becomes the declaration of your life.

Many of us have experienced hardship in life and been on the receiving end of maltreatment while all the blame for these circumstances belong to someone else. The majority of people come into contact with a victim's mentality, which says they are innocent bystanders to every event in life and negative incidents befall them by force. Then said individuals use this as a reason to not move forward or excel in life.

Let's be clear. Horrific circumstances do arise in which we cannot control . However, for many these things enter people's lives due to choices made. You have the power of choice. You get to choose what you are a part of, who you associate with, where you work and just about everything else in life ultimately you are in control.

It all boils down to choice. For, every decision carries consequences, for example if you pay your bill, your lights will remain on, if you should happen to choose not to pay the bill, the consequence is well, you will probably be eating in the dark. If you choose to continue hanging around those dysfunctional, chaotic and dramatic people you will continue to receive that same energy into your life.

Declare once again: **I AM NOT A VICTIM!**

It's true, you're not a victim. It's easy to place blame on everyone else when things are going wrong because it doesn't feel good to take responsibility for yourself and where you are in life especially if you aren't where you want to be in life. It all boils down to choice. If you don't like something in your life, **CHANGE IT**, don't blame, just make the needed changes. You are responsible for yourself and you are enjoying life. Stop giving other people control of your life, you're in control.

Being a victim is easy. It allows you to not be culpable for your actions or state of being. Stop blaming your weight or body shape on the food you eat. You ate it! Get up and go to the gym, start a diet or both. Stop blaming your finances on other people, you spent that money. You don't like your job, your pay, find a new job, ask for a raise. **IT'S YOUR CHOICE.**

Greatest weapon to fight against the victim mentality is a little thing called, **TAKING RESPONSIBILITY**. Examine your life. I'm sure, better yet I KNOW, you can and will find circumstances that you had no control over. I'm not suggesting that you accept blame for another person's wrong doings, but I am suggesting that you take the power away from that person, organization, event or by accepting what once happened, not wallowing in it, not allowing it to mislead you and move on. Moving on means you acknowledge the issue but the issue doesn't define you nor is it what you expect for your future and your kids, and their kids. Do your best to improve your life, situation and environment. The responsibility is yours. You are responsible for where you go from here. I know moving forward can be a very difficult thing, but you owe it to yourself to get up, dust yourself off and run. Run for your own life's sake.

DECLARE: I AM NOT A VICTIM!

Have you ever been a victim of the victim mentality?

What parts of your life are you unhappy with?

What changes do you need to make?

Describe what taking responsibility for your current state looks like.

What action steps can you take to move forward in your life?

Forgiveness

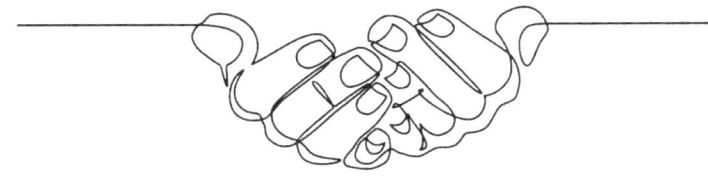

"For if ye forgive men their trespasses, your heavenly Father will also forgive you: But if ye forgive not men their trespasses, neither will your Father forgive your trespasses."

Matthew 6:14 & 15 (KJV)

Forgiveness is one of the most powerful weapons we have in our fight towards freedom, the future and overall life success. Forgiveness can be tough, but is essential. It is the key to unlock the door of yesterday, which opens to the corridor of tomorrow. The issue is these doors do not open at the same time. Many times we hang out in the doorway of yesterday looking at tomorrow, debating whether to cross the threshold. Your future holds vast potential, yet you will never arrive at your full capacity while carrying the antagonistic chains of the past.

We've all encountered cruel and unjust treatment, racism, called demeaning names, been lied to, cheated on, gone through divorce, break ups or unfairly fired from a job. Maybe worse, like experiencing the loss of someone's life, such as a family member or close friend and possibly at the hands of another person. You may have encountered some type of difficult situation in life, and whatever that situation is, you have to let it go. Easy to say, I know.

It's time to forgive those who have wronged you. You may even need to forgive yourself. I understand that this is easier said than done, especially if it still hurts or is an area of contention. One of the hardest things to do is to release emotional pain. The ones who hurt you don't deserve your forgiveness. However you need to forgive it regardless. Forgiveness is detrimental to your survival.

Think about what you have done to wrong someone at some point in your life. And maybe you or someone else felt you didn't deserve forgiveness. I imagine there are things you have done and don't realize or remember doing. We don't forgive for the sake of those villainous characters of the past, but on the contrary, we forgive for our own benefit. Selfish? Yes it is.

As long as you hold on to that emotional weight, you are held down and restricted, giving the culprit emotional control over you and your peace of mind. Triggering you with every whim. To live out your life's purpose effectively, you need to be, MUST be, **FREE!**

When you're tied to those emotions that are locked in past circumstances or issues, you make poor decisions and become socially broken. Jaded. I'm not advocating anyone being a doormat or anything like that. I'm also not a fan of the "forgive and forget" ideology either. You shouldn't forget what happened, but you shouldn't dwell upon it either. **Let the past be past, forgiveness is the fuel that moves your life vehicle forward.** You should take that past hurt and learn a lesson from what you've been through and apply it to your life. You have no idea who you will bless, encourage or help to gain freedom with the lessons you've learned.

When you forgive, you release yourself from the past and propel yourself toward your destiny. **STOP CARRYING THE BRICKS OF THE PAST**. When you carry bricks from the past you inevitably and eventually end up rebuilding your past in your present and future. Not only will you reside there but so will your children and maybe your children's children.

Many times people attempt to start new relationships, without resolving unforgiven past issues. More often than not the new relationship is just as tumultuous as the previous because they enter it with misguided and unhealthy expectations that have their roots and foundation in the past. The other person in this new relationship ends up being punished for the misfortunes of the old relationship. This is completely unfair and in a nutshell abuse of the other party. This applies to all areas of relationship.

Marriage/dating, business partnerships, employment, sports teams and even church. **If left unchecked, unforgiveness is just like termites eating away at the frame of a house, challenging its structural integrity**. Stop ignoring the issues, you can sweep them under the rug for so long until you have a mountain of garbage poking up in the center of the rug. Unforgiveness is a time bomb or more like a landmine. Anyone touches that area of your life and an explosion is bound to cause devastation. Acknowledged the issues, who it is that you need to forgive and move in freedom.

Declaration: (whenever you think about a situation or person, you need to forgive)

I choose to FORGIVE!

It may seem silly to recite this, and it may seem fake, but you have to continue until it becomes real to you. You will begin to feel freedom in every area that needs the healing of forgiveness. Whenever a person or situation comes to mind that needs to be resolved, just declare " I choose to forgive".

Who do you need to forgive?

What happened?

How long have you been harboring unforgiveness?

Are there things you need to forgive yourself for? What are those things?

Examine your Circle

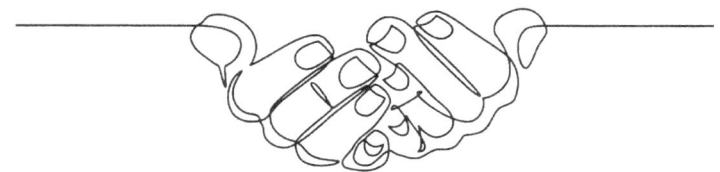

If you really want to know who a person is or what they are truly about. Just look at the people they surround themselves with.

You've heard the saying "guilty by association". Well that saying couldn't be more true, because you look like, sound like and act like whoever you spend the most time with, speaking of your character and internal views. Many times a group of friends will build or hold similar views, beliefs, mannerisms or appearances. This is why it is important to always examine your circle.

Those that dwell within your circle bring their accompanying thoughts, ideas and behaviors. This may explain why certain things in life look the way they do. When you are closely associated with dramatic people it seems as if problems never cease, likewise, if you are surrounded by successful people there is an impression left on your life that leans toward success. Now, think about the people you're connected to. Are they going where you want to go in life? Are they positive or negative? Lastly, do they hold the same or similar morals, ethics and values that you do?

I'm not suggesting you should be alone and have no friends or acquaintances. We all need friends, family and social interaction. I'm actually urging the use of wisdom in how we allow others to enter and influence your life. The effects others leave on your life will undoubtedly be passed on to someone else you're connected to, your children, spouse, co-workers etc.. Much like one rotten piece of fruit will ruin the bunch. Don't allow yourself to become ruined and then you begin to ruin others. But find relationships that heal, encourage and bring peace to your life, then pass those divine qualities onto others.

There are **THREE** types of people or relationships we should maintain in life.

People "above". Again not in a negative sense, but in the sense of mentorship/ leadership. This person, or these people are able to pour into your life. You are able to gain wisdom and insight from them.

People who are "equal". These people are the ones you have most in common with and have many similar ideas, beliefs and motives. These are the ones that help to sharpen you and can encourage you. You can tell this person anything, relate on a number of different levels and consistently grow.

People "beneath". Not in a derogatory sense, but in the sense that you should be pouring into someone else.

Teaching others how to overcome or to get to the level that you have made it to. You can't receive more than you pour out, the more you pour the more you receive.

The Relationhips Pyramid

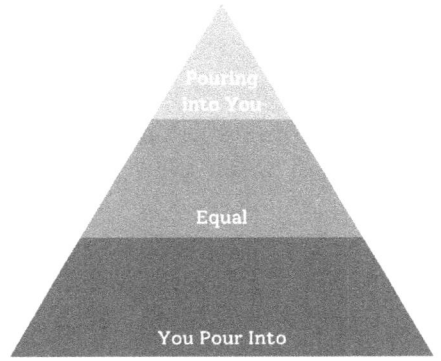

These 3 Relationships are paramount to your success and growth.

Corey Mangum

The idea someone pours into you, you mix with others and then, you pour into someone else. It's like a pyramid. The top should be narrow and grow wider towards the base. You don't want to, nor do you need too many voices speaking to you at a time. I can't stress this enough. Jesus knew this, he said "a house divided against itself can not stand"(Mark 3:25). Too many voices at some point will cause conflicting opinions to rise. Be careful who you let pour into you.

Be careful who you mingle with. Not everyone is interested in your success. Beware those who disguise themselves as equals yet become enemies via jealousy once you excel and they don't. **A true friend celebrates another's successes even during their time of struggle.**

Also not everyone deserves what you have to offer or pour out. The Bible warns in Matthew 7:6, not to cast our pearls before the swine. In other words, **don't give or offer your valuables to someone who does not understand nor appreciate its value**.

In proper alignment this all works and flows downward. Top to bottom.

Who are the 5 you spend most of your time interacting with?

1. _____

2. _____

3. _____

4. _____

5. _____

Where are these people in your pyramid? Categorize the above 5.

Top (Pouring into you):

Middle (Equal):

Bottom(Pouring into them):

Who do you need to limit your interactions with?

Possible virtual mentors.

1. _____

2. _____

3. _____

Traits you see in others you admire that you would like to adopt.

1. _____

2. _____

3. _____

The Other's

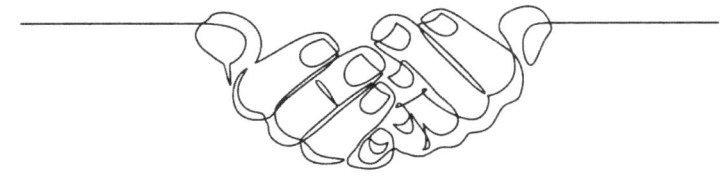

"Joseph had a dream. When he told it to his brothers, they hated him even more".

Genesis 37:5 MSG

People will love you for you and hate you for success.

People will love you for you and hate you for success. Much like when you fail. Everyone wants to hang around you when you're winning but they are quick to jump ship when you're losing. No one wants to be the person to help pick up the pieces, at your lowest points, you often find yourself alone.

Success is attractive and alluring, yet breeds contempt from those who lost it, for those who have obtained it. Haters come with the territory. Believe it or not there are some people out there who don't want you to succeed, and some hope and wish for your demise. These haters usually aren't strangers. You've probably shared a meal with these people, or grown up in the same house, or maybe you currently go to the same church or school. Your haters are closer than you think.

It's of the utmost importance that you have a healthy understanding of success and why you want it. If you desire the approval, attention and praise of others as your mark of success you want to reassess. The praise of mankind is fleeting, looking for the next, newest, loudest big thing. As long as you're entertaining or pleasing to them they'll be with you, support you,or join your cause, but the second your interest no longer aligns that support vanishes like mist.

If you do, whatever you do, for the praise and attention of others, you have your reward already. But what if that praise never comes?

Set your affection/desires on greater things, find a greater drive, seek a higher form of accomplishment. Challenge yourself to maximize your efforts and chase generational blessings and lasting legacy which will live on even after you've transitioned.

People will love you for you, but hate you for success. The reasons for this are jealousy, greed and envy. Such ugliness. People hate your vision because they hate the thought of where they will be when you achieve it. No one wants to be left behind. It's not you, so don't take it personal, they don't know how to manage emotions nor do they possess the ambition to change their station in life. They are upset that they didn't have the courage to chase their dreams. Don't you apologize for that either. Oftentimes we make excuses and compensate for other people's behavior and then compromise our wellbeing for their comfort. **DO NOT NOT SHRINK YOURSELF TO FIT OTHER PEOPLE'S EXPECTATIONS.**

You know the saying, "misery loves company". It's true, as long as you remain in the same state you've been in you're sure to maintain those same relationships. Misfortune and Victimhood are familiar and widely accepted, even expected by most people. A person living in victory in every area of life is unfamiliar and difficult to welcome into the fold of common individuals.

Much like the young man Joseph from the Bible, who's vision and desires of success created occasion for his brothers (those closest to him) to hate him. They threw him into a pit, cut his precious coat and sold him into slavery. All this because of the favor in his life and the astounding dream he dreamt.

Joseph's brothers mocked him, plotted to kill him, stripped him, threw him into a pit and then took a lunch break, sat down to eat as if it was just another normal day at the office. All of this because of his envisioned success and where they would be once the dream came to pass. They resented him for the dream and the idea of him possibly ruling over them. Beyond how others will treat you because of your dream, there is another lesson to learn.

BE CAREFUL WHO YOU TELL YOUR DREAMS TO. Not everyone is mature enough to handle your dreams. Some attempt to cast fear and doubt into your dream because they don't possess the foresight or faith required to see something so amazing come to pass.

Don't be surprised when you are abandoned by those you thought were closest to you, and you expected to celebrate your victories with you. You're not doing it for them anyway. Your sights are set higher than they can comprehend. Your affections are set above that of theirs and other people.

People will love you for you and hate you for success.

Success is attractive

Other people will be attracted to your success and desire to be in proximity to you. It's not necessarily you that they're after, but what you offer and what they think they can get. Potiphar, Pharaoh's officer and captain of the guard, had a wife who was hot on Joseph's trail after seeing the favor and success in his life, attempted to get him to have an affair with her. She had eyes for what was lofty. She made several solicitations toward him to sleep with her yet he rejected every one. One day when they were alone in the house she grabbed him by his clothes attempting to force him but he ran out, with a piece of his clothes in her hand. Her word against his was that he had attempted to sleep with her. Now we know this was untrue but Potiphar believed it and had Joseph locked up in prison.

Your success can attract people, it's up to you to determine which people are right for you to connect to. Some want to use you to fulfill their selfish motives and pleasures.

If you are able to withstand the pressure and remain focused. In the end you will be a blessing to many. Many need what you have to offer and don't know it but their future and survival may depend upon the fruition of your dreams or vision. Just like the story of Joseph. There was a famine in the land and his brothers went to Egypt to seek provisions, there they found Joseph healthy and full of life. Joseph was their relief as he was able to help them in their time of crisis. People will value your visions when they are able to reap the benefits.

Genesis 50:20, In the story of Joseph and his brothers. Joseph makes such a profound statement to his brother. Upon their fathers death they feared that Joseph would seek retaliation against them for all of the things they did to him. The profound statement he made was " You plotted evil against me, but God turned it into good, in order to preserve the lives of many people who are alive today because of what happened." This is a reminder not to taint the blessing of the Lord with vengeance. Never stoop to a fool's level.

Have you told your dreams to people who you shouldn't have? What was the outcome?

Did you keep chasing or give up due to fear and doubt or possibility of criticism?

How do you personally navigate the praises and attention of others?

Have you ever found yourself captivated by the attention of others?

Have you had people turn on you?

How did you handle it?

Stay on the Wall

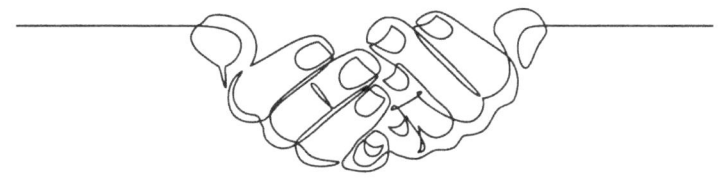

So I sent messengers to them, saying, "I am doing a great work and cannot come down. Why should the work stop while I leave to come down to [meet with] you?" Nehemiah 6:3 (AMP)

The Enemy's Plot

6 Now when it was reported to Sanballat, Tobiah, Geshem the Arab, and to the rest of our enemies that I had rebuilt the wall, and *that* no breach was left in it, although at that time I had not installed the doors in the gates, 2 Sanballat and Geshem sent *a message* to me, saying, "Come, let's meet together [a]at Chephirim in the plain of Ono." But they were plotting to [b]harm me. 3 So I sent messengers to them, saying, "I am doing a great work and am unable to come down. Why should the work stop while I leave it and come down to you?" 4 Then they sent *messages* to me four times worded in this way, and I answered them with the same wording.

In this life, we've all been given work to do. Some people just haven't come into the realization or revelation of their work yet. However, for those who have, I want to remind you and encourage you, to *stay on the wall.*

The Wall: The wall represents the work that you have been dedicated to in an effort to see your hopes, dreams and vision come to life. The Wall equals legacy. What you will leave behind at your passing. Hold your position. Keep up the good work. Keep striving for success.

When you gain an understanding of legacy and the importance of your work, you begin to realize why you do what you do. Many have a vision or dream of what the future holds. They can smell it, taste it, hear it, and even feel it. **Faith!**

As strong as your desire is, is just how strong distractions will be, opposing said desire. When mapping out success most people don't account for distractions and the battles that may rise along the way. It's inevitable. Once you begin and you put your hands to work, every possible reason in the world for you to stop will show up, some yelling in your face, some whispering in your ear. Don't let them steal your attention. **Stay on the wall.**

One great tool to measure the quality, effectiveness and impact of your work is to weigh it against the amount of things attempting to pull you away from the work.

Without fail, when you're making progress, something of "equal" importance comes along to steal your attention.

Yet remember this is just a distraction from the greater work you have committed your hands to. More than likely that time is of temporary importance, someone else can handle it. You're busy investing in the future. This is where you must set priorities.

Priorities

Setting levels of priority and importance is a major key to success. Without priorities completion is virtually impossible. When your priorities are set inconsequential matters remain to be just that,insignificant. There is a certain value assigned to the work at hand and its completion. Long lasting generational implications outweigh short term satisfaction of giving into distractions.

I encourage you to read the book of Nehemiah, found in the Bible. In it you will find his story, about repairing the wall that surrounded his beloved city. This was vital work which would impact a nation and several generations to come.

Now as Nehemiah is hard at work, Sanballat, Tobiah, Geham and the rest of his nation's enemies heard about the work that was being done so they sent messages to Nehemiah to stop his work and to come meet with them. However they only desired to harm him. **It's a set up.**

Its a set up

There are things that you have been working on or need to work on in an effort to heal, repair just better you and your family, breaking generational curses, shortcomings, and issues. Building financial wealth, creating educational standards, or whatever you can name. Only you really know what your family needs. Whatever it may be, there will always be something or someone who is an enemy to your progress, attempting to lure you away from the work. **It's a set up!**

I like Nehemiah's response to his distractors. In verses 2 &3 he says "I know they just want to hurt me". So he sent back a message saying "I'm doing a great a work here, I can't come down", ``why should the work cease or come to a standstill just for me to come see you?" **Stay on the wall.**

He recognized the threat the distraction posed to the success of him and his people, likewise you must recognize the threats that rise against you and your people. Peace, joy and destiny are depending on you to remain firm. Look at that distraction, ask yourself, is it pushing me towards the outcome I've dreamt or pulling me back into ruin? **Stay on the wall!**

Describe your wall (Your life's work—legacy you are building)

What distractions have you been facing?

Have you established a plan of response for distractions?

What is the plan? If you have no plan, create one below.

Who or what are you working for? (Your Why)

Don't give up on your dream.

It's still in the construction phase.

Keep working.

-Corey Mangum

Self Discipline

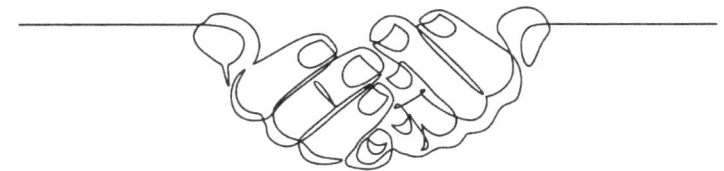

He that hath no rule over his own spirit is like a city that is broken down, and without walls. Proverbs 25:28 KJV

Self Discipline- The ability to control one's feelings, actions and overcome one's weaknesses. The ability to pursue that which one thinks is right despite the temptation to abandon it.

Synonyms: Self control, will power or restraint
Many people are unable to achieve, maintain or produce success due to a lack of **SELF DISCIPLINE**. Many are compulsive. Acting solely or majorly upon compulsive behavior is considered to be a mental and behavioral health disorder, when left unchecked. It is thoughts and urges manifest that persist despite the negative effects on one's health, employment, relationships and own personal wellbeing.

Self Discipline is the remedy for many of the issues, problems and negative situations you face daily. If you had the Self discipline to stay the course you would be living a different outcome.

When I say self discipline, I don't mean self punishment or consequence. I'm talking about creating structure or a plan and sticking to it. Many people want to lose weight, quit smoking/drinking or get a degree,etc.. Yet lack of discipline hinders those desires from becoming reality. Achieving life changing accomplishments and goals requires more than DESIRE and PRAYER, action, continual action is necessary.

Action is needed even when you don't feel like it. Act!

Every year, on January 1st, we make our "New Year's Resolution", yet approximately 80% of all those resolutions fail by the second week of February. Why? Let's take weight loss for example. That diet plan was easy to find online, the supplements are bought and paid for, you purchased the gym membership, all because the desire to chase was so strong. Once the beauty and splendor of desire fades you're left with stuff. You go to the gym for a few weeks then other things start to lead you to second guess your ambitions and desires.

Self Discipline is to forgo instant gratification in reach of long term gain. That means when it hurts, when it's hard and when you come to that fork in the road, pointing you to give up or keep going. **You keep GOING!**. You have to overcome the temptation to quit or go back to what you used to be. When speaking at a juvenile detention center, I told the youth there, if you don't discipline yourself someone else will. Which is what landed the majority of them in the situation they were in. If you aren't disciplined you'll receive punishment, or consequences that feel like the punishment. There are natural consequences to every action that we take or refrain from taking. Discipline helps to protect us from those consequences.

It's all about the mind and the choices we make. Stop choosing things that aren't in your best interest or that go against your goals, dreams and self respect. People who lack self discipline often lack self respect and confidence. It's a tough road but you will be extremely happy with the results.

Proverbs 15:32

Self discipline is something you will have to work at daily. Everyone. Even that person that you see who looks like they win in every phase of life gets the urge to quit, stop short or do the opposite of what is right for them. Just know you can do it. Failure is not an option.

Self Discipline can be correlated with **SELF LOVE**. When you disciple yourself you are provided a certain level of self-love. What does this look like? Love protects, heals, and operates in the best interest of those it's aimed towards. A lack of Self Discipline, is Self Harm. If you can't or won't discipline yourself you are the one to blame for your situation.

Discipline is a proactive approach to success. Discipline is not the reaction to failure. Rather, discipline establishes the standards that protect you there from. Don't feel like going to the gym? Go anyway. Don't like reading? Read anyway. Don't feel like waking up early? **GET UP AND MAKE IT HAPPEN ANYWAY!** No one can do it for you.

DISCIPLINE IS THE KEY!

Where do you lack discipline?

1. _____

2. _____

3. _____

4. _____

5. _____

What actions do you need to take, that you have been avoiding?

1. _____

2. _____

3. _____

4. _____

5. _____

Write a letter to yourself about how you have been and how you are going to be moving forward concerning your level of Self-Discipline.

Redefine Risk (Risk pt.2)

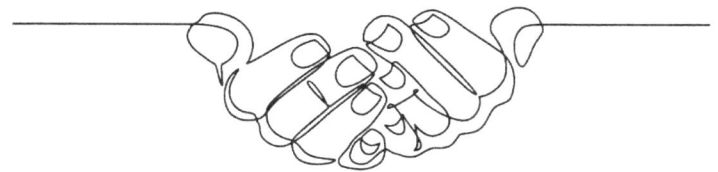

We previously talked about risk and taking risk but I think it very important to examine our definition of what risk is.

Risk is the exposure to possible harm or danger. Risk is taking action or <u>not</u> taking action with the possibility of loss or great gain or return on the original investment.

When we talk about risk we typically see it from a negative perception. Why is this? Well I'm glad you asked. The reason for this negative connotation is: we've been conditioned to seek and remain in a place of comfort. We have been trained to fall into a system and remain in the familiar with no expectation for great unless given permission from the system. We have been trained to live, and think within a box. That box has been fashioned to fulfill our minimum comforts.

Your sense of comfort is your single greatest enemy to growth. If something stretches you beyond the realm of normalcy or convenience, you more than likely reject or avoid it at all costs. The truth about comfort is that it creates complacency and more often than not, stagnation. When was the last time you did something new or outside of your comfort zone?

Take a class?

Read a book?

Meet a new person?

Apply for a job?

Exercise?

Eat a new food?

ANYTHING......

Inactivity is extremely risky and more dangerous to your life's success than actions that provide you chances to make something good or new happen in your life.

Fear and doubt have held you hostage long enough. It's time for you to take your authority back. No one can do this for you. Just like investing in your future. The more you invest, the more you can expect as a return.

You're sick of your job and most of the people you work with; but fear, doubt and comfort talked you out of applying for your dream job. For years you've held on to the dream of starting your own business, working for yourself and creating freedom for generations to come. You've been telling yourself year after year that you ought to go back to school but make up every excuse known to man as to why you can't make a move.

You have to retrain your brain to redefine what risk really is and look at the actions you're taking, or the lack thereof, due to an unhealthy understanding of risk. When you understand risk you recognize the danger of losing your dreams and ambitions because of the lack of required action. Any and everything that you've accomplished thus far, required you to take a risk. There were many unknown variables before it all worked out. We can go down a very long list, from your employment to relationships to sports and even driving your car.

Sit down and write out your vision, create a step by step action plan for peak execution of the vision. This will help you to manage the associated risks. Risks are always present. The reward most certainly outweighs the risks.

What action(s) have you put off for a fear of the risks involved?

Describe how you will feel on the other side of the risk.

How will your life look if you take the chance?

What steps can you take to move forward from here?

Persistence

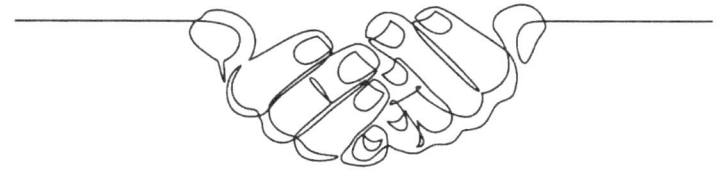

Luke 18:2-8 KJV

2 Saying, There was in a city a judge, which feared not God, neither regarded man:

3 And there was a widow in that city; and she came unto him, saying, Avenge me of mine adversary.

4 And he would not for a while: but afterward he said within himself, Though I fear not God, nor regard man;

5 Yet because this widow troubleth me, I will avenge her, lest by her continual coming she weary me.

6 And the Lord said, Hear what the unjust judge saith.

7 And shall not God avenge his own elect, which cry day and night unto him, though he bear long with them?

8 I tell you that he will avenge them speedily. Nevertheless when the Son of man cometh, shall he find faith on the earth?

In the above mentioned scriptures in Luke 18, in some Bible versions there is a caption which reads the story of the persistent widow. One version says in verse 5 that the widow was wearing the judge out or annoying him and one said that he was scared that she would beat him black and blue if he continued to ignore her request. The power of persistence.

A persistent person is a dangerous person.

A persistent person is a dangerous person. The true test of your faith isn't this mystic idea that you believe in or for something, it's the actions that support your belief. Faith requires action. If you lack faith, you lack action, and if you lack action, you lack faith. Faith without work associated with it is dead.(Read, **James 2:26 KJV—look below).** No one can question your level of faith if you are working in pursuit of something but when you're stagnant, your faith is called into suspicion. When Jesus' disciples lacked movement to accomplish a task, He simply said "oh yeah of little faith". This occurred several times in the Bible. For instance, when Jesus rebuked the storm (Matthew 8:26), fear fell upon the disciples, who became stagnate and overcome with thoughts of despair. At the moment, the task or goal seems great, but persistence says you will achieve it if you stick with it.

It's rare to find a person willing to persevere through adverse winds, but if you give up now, you'll stop short of the goal and will be left stranded in the middle of the sea. **You've come too far to quit**. Keep moving forward. As you consistently press forward you will find strength and muscle of character begin to develop within you. Adversity can be extremely uncomfortable and inconvenient, but it will make you stronger if you fight through it.

I suggest you read Luke 18:1-8 there, Jesus is speaking about prayer and how to not waver in your persistence in making a request. However we can't relegate this idea to just asking but also the way we chase after our dreams, visions, and wants. Anything you desire you can have if you are willing to fight for it. Many people are quick to give up at the first sign of trouble or the instance they hear "no". You have to be the person who craves the nos, the more you hear no, the closer you are getting to yes. Procrastination, fear and lack of confidence are overcome by your persistence. A persistent person is a dangerous person. No one can stop a man or woman who is persistent, they are not easily deterred from their goals, they are unlikely to retreat yet likely to continue to advance no matter the obstacle in their path.

In the mind of a persistent person, there is no other option. They don't have to be coaxed into giving it their all. They just do it.

I'm sure you've heard the saying, "how do you eat an elephant? One bite at a time". Well this is the attitude of the persistent. No matter how big the goal, obstacle, task or mission, I can get this done one step/bite at a time. A persistent person is a dangerous person. If you are in their way, be prepared to get run over or left in their dust. In

Luke 11:5-10, Jesus is talking to his Disciples about prayer. Not just pray but persistence in prayer. A man comes to his neighbors house at midnight asking for food to feed his guests but the homeowner refuses to answer because he's in bed. But something interesting happens in Verse 8. The owner is disturbed and his resistance worn down by his neighbors persistence that he answers the door and gives the man whatever he needs or wants. You have to maintain the same attitude. Ask, ask, and ask again. Chase, chase and chase again. Resubmit your application, business plan, or legal docs. Reschedule that meeting. Go back to school. Get back on your diet. Whatever that thing is for you, **GO FOR IT AND DON'T GIVE UP!!!**

A persistent person is a dangerous person. People are uncomfortable around determined, focused, persistent people, because these attributes are uncommon. You know who is the best example of persistence? Your kid. The one that asks and asks and will probably do it anyway, even after 5 no's. There is no other option in their mind. They know what they want and go after it.—Disobeying parents isn't OK, I'm just trying to make a point (you get it).

A persistent person is resilient. A person who has set their mind to achieve whatever it is they desire and go after no matter what life throws at them. You may get knocked down, but bounce back and get back to it. You might not feel like you're at 100% all the time, you may fall short or make a mistake. Don't wallow in your shortcomings. Life will always offer resistance to your persistence, but, if it's worth having, it's worth fighting for. You will have to fight self doubt, discomfort, tiredness, physical or emotional pain, loneliness and fear. But you hang in there. **You can overcome it!**

Don't allow difficulty to deter you from reaching your goals. Your mind must be set on achievement mode. You have to become dangerous to all opposition. Nothing can stand in the way of you and your mountain top. You're the king or queen of the hill. If you find it easy to give up because of gossip, being treated unfairly, lack of support or just poor circumstances in general. Know that **YOU CAN DO IT**. Remind yourself of your goals, constantly. Sit and meditate on the outcomes, see yourself in a place of success and achievement. Create a list of things that will happen based upon your achievement of your goals. Make the end results so real that you can smell it, taste it, hear it and feel it. You have more power within you than you realize. Become dangerous. **BE PERSISTENT**

"Oh ye of little faith" Matthew 6:30, Matthew 8:26, Matthew 16:8, Luke 12:28

James 2:26
26. For as the body without the spirit is dead, so faith without works is dead also.

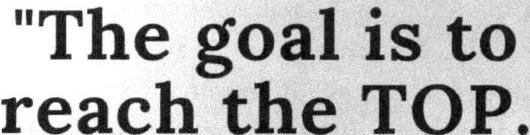

"The goal is to reach the TOP.

-DON'T STOP-

Consistency is the key".

Corey
Mangum

Reminder—BE YOURSELF

Now if you don't take heed to, digest, receive or accept anything else from this book. **PLEASE**, embrace this part. One of the most important things I can or will ever write and one of the greatest lessons taught to me was to **"BE YOURSELF"**.

I know there's another portion of the book with some of the same subject matter, but this topic is of the utmost importance for your life. Knowing you is key to unlocking the life you desire, recovering from trauma and bettering yourself or circumstances.

In this current world and time in our existence there is so much pressure to do, be and to have what other people do or have. In our society there is a massive amount of duplicate copies and a lack of authentic originals. This is part of the surge in "reality TV'. people are hungry for the real, unique and something different. But in the chase for that many attempt to disguise themselves as what they see and those who entertain them.

How can you do what you were created and born to do if you're not being you?

There is so much reward in life from being yourself. Freedom is upon those who are true to who they really are. Freedom means not bound nor slave to. Suppressing your identity and wearing another's. Free from a perpetual Halloween, constantly wearing a mask of someone else's face, personality, like or dislikes. You or someone you know has even set their likes and dislikes based upon someone else's preferences. That's a sad existence.

This instant gratification culture has caused so many to chase what they see and to make that the standard of living. Most people can't handle the cost of living at the level they see on TV. Some are unable to survive the pressures required to keep with what they see.

Sad truth is that depression, fear, anxiety and many forms of addiction are the result of this bondage of lack of self identity and oftentimes will lead to death.

BE YOURSELF!

Players & Fans

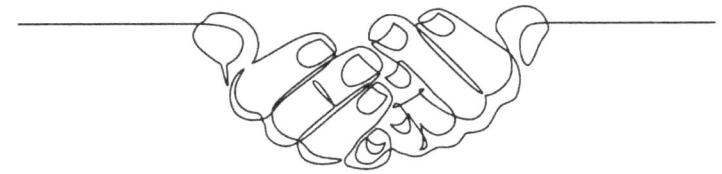

I want you to think about two types of people. Players and fans. It's amazing to think about all of the things that we've witnessed in sports history. We've seen the greatest of the greats and we're watching the evolution of many sports as time progresses. People are physically able to do things that were beyond the imagination of those who started many of the sports we watch today. It's always fun to watch the best of the best in professional sports do what they do best. Watching All Star games and highlight reels, cause such excitement and an adrenaline rush to serge, leading our memories back to our personal glory days and the imaginations of an older generation to a place of feeling like we "still got it".

There are so many things that players and fans have in common, yet many things that set them apart.

Both players and fans can wear jerseys, shoes, sit in the arenas and more, but it's what sets them apart from one another that makes the difference. Before we go any further I want you to know, I'm a fan, I love sports, I love to watch all the terrific plays made, I love to watch all the different dunks and the touchdowns, and the celebrations that follow. I love to watch the champions get their rings. But I'm just a fan.

As a fan you watch the players play their games. You pay a price to watch them play, whether live or pay per view or some streaming service. You wear a jersey, hat or some other sport paraphernalia which the player also wears. You have the keychain and you're loyal to the team. Win, lose or draw, you remain a fan and you're not jumping ship. Matter of fact you can bash on your team, but if anyone else says a negative word about the team they may have to meet you in a parking lot and square up (fight) with you.

Being a fan can be healthy and can help to produce a level of expectation or desire within. The danger is being mind locked in the identity of a fan and paralyzed therein. We see people in constant arguments about whose team is better as if there is a vested interest in the team. It's fun to watch your favorite team win. But you are just a fan.

We need more people in our world to cross the road from the fans side to the players side. Players actually get in the game. Tons of people are on the sidelines of life watching others make great plays and accomplishments wishing they were able to do it or judging how they did it, yet never applying themselves to even trying to accomplish what the player of life has. The player has paid the price of their blood, sweat and tears into their craft and that much more to win a championship. It's time to stop the fanship and get into the game.

Most people talk a "good game", especially at the beginning of the year. All resolutions, motivational books and videos along with all those social media posts pumping you up. You post about how great you are and all the changes you're about to make, how you're about to make it happen. Well enough talk. Put your pads on, put your cleats on, lace up your sneakers, it's time to get moving. It's time to get in the game. You can remain a fan your entire life and watch as things happen for others and nothing happens for you, or you can get up and make some major decisions and put in the work and see greatness come to life for you.

Many players, though rivals, are fans of each other. You can certainly be a fan and player at the same time. You can cheer for others and still be in the game. Matter of fact it's encouraged and is healthy. It's those critical people we don't play, have never played and don't understand the game who you must be leary of.

You ought to be dunking on people in success, you ought to be hitting home runs in achievements, you ought to be setting new records and crushing old ones, you ought to be setting new trends, you ought to be the one who's hitting monumental levels. Realize people are waiting on you, somebody's waiting on you to make the difference to get in the game. You're not the MVP in your own life right now, because you haven't gotten in the game. You've been sitting on the sidelines all this time and it's time to get in the game.

The sidelines are crowded. The arena is packed. There's a limited number of players on the court/field at a time. So you have to rise to the level of playing in the game.

It's time to decide, are you a player or a fan?

Poverty's Associates/Causes

Go to the ant, you sluggard; consider its ways and be wise! It has no commander, no overseer or ruler, yet it stores its provisions in summer and gathers its food at harvest. How long will you lie there, you sluggard? When will you get up from your sleep? A little sleep, a little slumber, a little folding of the hands to rest and poverty will come on you like a thief and scarcity like an armed man.

Proverbs 6:6-11NIV

I went by the field of the slothful, and by the vineyard of the man void of understanding; And, lo, it was all grown over with thorns, and nettles had covered the face thereof, and the stone wall thereof was broken down. Then I saw, and considered it well: I looked upon it, and received instruction. Yet a little sleep, a little slumber, a little folding of the hands to sleep: So shall thy poverty come as one that travelleth; and thy want as an armed man.

Proverbs 24:30-34 KJV

Poverty is an uncomfortable state to be in, it goes beyond one's financial status and extends into their mindset and character. The way that a person carries themselves tells a lot about their proximity to poverty. Poverty affects not only one's finances but their mental and physical health, personal and professional relationships and other areas of life.

The poverty mindset is always looking for a hand out, making an excuse as to why they can't. Consuming while never producing. Entitled and abusive towards those closest to them. Poverty and prosperity mindsets are both taught and neither is easily broken. To change your mindset you have to unlearn poor thinking and surround yourself with the opposite. This holds true for anything in life that you desire to learn and unlearn.

Let's look at a few attributes that can be associated with poverty.

Laziness and Indolence
Those who avoid action, effort and work will always find poverty.

Lover of Pleasure
Those who chase pleasure will spend all they have to get it, and poverty awaits them.

Lack of Discipline
Those who lack discipline and self restraint are easily drawn away from what truly matters.

Drunkenness

Those given to Drunkenness lose the ability to make sound decisions which leads to poverty.

Unhealthy associations / affiliations/ relationships

Those relationships can be a hemorrhage to your life.

Lack of Vision

Those who walk through life void of vision are limited in the heights they can reach.

Trying to keep up with the lifestyle of others. Allowing people to leech your increase. Peer pressure to be or have something, will lead to a lack filled life. Attempting to buy love, attention and affection. Escaping reality, wandering through life with any sense of direction, are all surefire ways to live in an impoverished state(financial, emotional, spiritual, mental and relational).

To avoid poverty, avoid the above mentioned characteristics.

Many are comfortable with living in a state of poverty. Escaping this status requires hard work and effort. It is easy to sit back and demand things but it can be difficult putting in the work required to make the changes needed to escape the poverty mindset and lifestyle. Saving money, fighting your own desire for instant gratification and running from responsibility are all sure ways to miss out on quality opportunities to excel.

A person who is constantly attempting to grow and avoid poverty in every area of their life is focused on avoiding those things that will lead to their destruction. Proverbs 14:12 "There is a way *that seems* right to a man, But its end *is* the way of death."

Laziness is a lack of work and motivation thereof. 2 Thessalonians 3:10

10. "For even when we were with you, this we commanded you, that if any would not work, neither should he eat." It amazes me how there are so many people who want the rewards of hard work but refuse to actually work. These are those people who look at the accomplishments and gains of others and say "must be nice" in a sarcastic and cynical manner.

Pleasure. Pleasure in and of itself is not bad. There are things available to us that provide a sense of pleasure and satisfaction. This is a good thing. No one should walk through life miserable, void of joy and not experiencing any of the pleasures of life. That said, those who throw away restraint and wisdom and become chasers of pleasure won't be successful. Proverbs 21:17King James Version "He that loveth pleasure shall be a poor man: he that loveth wine and oil shall not be rich." We see those who are wealthy and successful and to our eyes life looks so easy and pleasurable and I'm sure it is, but much discomfort and sacrifice comes before pleasure. Many have a habit of spending all that they have on pleasure and at the end are left empty as pleasure only lasts a moment.

Discipline. The lack of Discipline is a killer to all progress. Discipline keeps one on the path of success. When you want to give up or stop discipline steadys your feet and focus. Discipline sets order and boundaries for your life and leads you away from all forms of chaos. Self discipline keeps you moving when motivation wears off. As distractions come you will be able to avoid them and perform at your greatest level of ability when you are disciplined.

Drunkenness. The cost(financial) of drinking and consumption of drugs is so high, that alone should be reason enough to stay away. A habitual state of drunkenness or drug induced high often causes a codependency with a substance, in which the dependent loses regard for all things except their substance of choice. Families, marriages and careers have been destroyed by drunkenness. We see celebrities who seem to have it all, lose it all in what seems to be a moment or blink of an eye. Inhibitions are lowered and a person is capable of unimaginable things, things they swore they would never do. Drunkenness leaves one empty and void of any kind of fulfillment. Throwing one's earnings, health and time away is dangerous to success.

Vision. You have to know what you want and where you want to go in life. If not, you're wondering. Directionless people can not, and do not prosper. It is those who process the foresight of hope and the future who achieve great success. Those who walk through life aimless will inevitably meet their demise.

Proverbs 29:18 King James Version18 "Where there is no vision, the people perish: but he that keepeth the law, happy is he."

The lack of vision allows distractions to lay siege to and captivate your focal interests. Where vision is missing, direction and focus are dead. Faith without vision is not faith. Faith in something requires you to have a vision for that thing, it becomes something to strive for. You may not physically see it, but you are able to see it in your mind's eye. Vision in cooperation with Discipline makes for a dangerous person, and one of victory.

Associations. Whoever you choose to spend time with matters. Those you associate/and spend quantities of time with have the ability to influence you most. Your decision making is greatly impacted by those you intermingle with. My mother has a saying: "water seeks its own level". Many of the negative associations people have are maintained out of a lack of self confidence, inability to see self as the royal that they are or the belief that they don't belong at a higher level of existence. Poverty follows poverty, just like wealth, prosperity and rich follow each other. Your association will serve as examples and you will follow said examples.

Poverty is simply lacking in one's life. Lack in ANY area of life. Instead of a lack filled life we should prescribe abundant life.

In what area(s) of life do you lack?

What area(s) of life have you noticed a leak in your wealth? (Wealth: Mental, financial and physical health.)

How do you protect yourself from poverty's association?

What did your parents/school teach you about prosperity?

Who do you associate with to help elevate your thinking from poverty to prosperity?

Weekend/Freetime

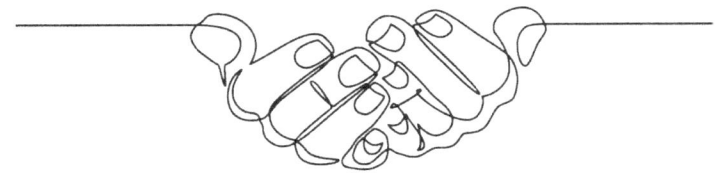

The Lord is my shepherd; I shall not want. He maketh me to lie down in green pastures: he leadeth me beside the still waters. He restoreth my soul: he leadeth me in the paths of righteousness for his name's sake. Yea, though I walk through the valley of the shadow of death, I will fear no evil: for thou art with me; thy rod and thy staff they comfort me. Thou preparest a table before me in the presence of mine enemies: thou anointest my head with oil; my cup runneth over. Surely goodness and mercy shall follow me all the days of my life: and I will dwell in the house of the Lord for ever.

Psalm 23 KJV

Time is your most precious commodity. Time is rare. So rare in fact that once gone it will never come back. Every moment that passes is irreplaceable. This is why we hear so many say, "use your time wisely", this includes the weekend or your freetime. Many people will tell you, "you better grind" "no days off" "no such thing as a weekend".

Well that may work for some people, but some just can't hang. Creating a perfect balance between weekend fun, time with family and friends, and resting is needed. You have to learn the difference. Not all freetime is lounge time or sleepy rest time, however it's not always grind time.

Imagine if you spent the entire weekend on the "grind" giving no attention to your spouse or children. Better yet what if they did that to you? I'm sure someone is reading this thinking: if only, or thank you for leaving me alone and not buggin me. Not gonna lie, ME TOO! That's a funny thought, but after so long it would become bothersome and leave you with a feeling of neglect or abandonment.

Use my 3 R's of the weekend **REST**, **RECOVER** and **REVIEW**.

REST—Just what it sounds like. Get some! Rest is vital to your survival. Do something to release you after that long stressful work week. Relaxation will help you to avoid burnout which causes many to give up on their dreams and ambitions. When you are unrested you make for a horrible person to communicate with and your decision making abilities are trash. Rest is often overlooked as an important key to success. If you are burnt out and lack energy you can't move the line of progress forward. When you are engulfed in your work, it can be easy to plug away and over work yourself, not getting the rest you need. Lack of rest has been correlated with sickness and mental health issues. Once you fall ill it becomes harder to get work done and your body attempts to force you into a place where you must rest so that it can heal. Your work and dreams need you to be healthy!

Recover—Release any harmful or negative thoughts and emotions that may have followed you from your normal work week. Not every day is sunshine, cake and ice cream. Jesus said in John 16:33 "we would have trouble in this world" and he was absolutely right. But we don't have to carry those troubles all throughout our existence. Jesus goes on to say, "be of good cheer I have overcome the world and its troubles". Much like a person who has gone through surgery, after they have been cut open, they are moved to recovery to begin the healing process and recover from the trauma of the operation. Your mental, physical and emotional facilities are in need of recovery from all of the pressures they have experienced recently. Many of your experiences have come to help you grow, develop your character and maybe perfect your faith, much like an athlete who uses weights and exercises in the same manner. You and the athlete have to take a rest period, whether that's in between sets, days, projects or any other time frame. You need to recover. In the time of recovery you are able to be restored. The 23rd psalm talks about being restored, "He makes me lie down in green pasture, leads me beside the still waters, He restores my soul". Sounds like recovery to me. In the green pasture you can be fed and well nourished, the still water will hydrate you and you will ultimately be restored. I can't tell you how long to rest in the place of recovery, only you can determine what is best for you. But I encourage you to recover. Boxers have a time to recover between every round for about a matter of minutes, and find recovery. In recovery pray for a release, meditate on the positive and choose to forgive, yes, forgive.

Review—Review your week or progress. What were the intended plans or goals? What went well, what didn't go so well? Where did you improve and what could you have done better or different. What lessons did you learn? Reflection is an essential part of your growth and what better time to reflect than when you are in your resting and recovery time? When you review during the working process (which is important to do), you will oftentimes overthink an issue or an idea, review and reflection when unoccupied can help to create clarity in your thoughts.

This is really a time for preplanning. What does my next week look like? What goal can I set for the next week, month, or year? Maybe even two to five years out. What adjustments do I need to make to my current goals or ideas? This is where you set the tone for your back to the grind phase. This is also when we refocus the why. Remember why these goals or ideas are so important to you. You wanted to accomplish these things for a reason, go back to review those reasons. Focus on your why and let it be your driving force.

Get some Rest, Recover from previous stresses, and Review how you did and how you're going to move forward. Sleep, vacation, cleaning, reading, going for a walk or to the gym. I can't tell you how to rest or for how long, but understand you need to do so as often as necessary and possible. You're not at your best if you're not rested and recovered nor have a sense of direction.

What type of things do you often need rest from?

What activities best help you to feel refreshed?

Do you have regular scheduled rest, relaxation focus time? When is it?

How often do you review your goals?

Building a business is **HARD**

Marriage is **HARD**

Investing is **HARD**

Exercise is **HARD**

Learning new skills is **HARD**

Getting a degree is **HARD**

Stop letting **"HARD"**
outweigh **WORTH**

The Fight of Your Life

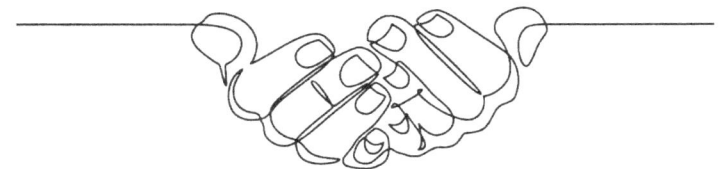

It's time for you to accomplish your goals and push yourself to the limit. You're able to do more than you realize. Stretch yourself into growth. Get up and make it happen. Oh I hear you saying "it's too hard", "I'm beyond the point of change" or "it's too late for me, I'm too old". Well as long as you keep telling yourself those lies, they will remain your truth. Stop lying to yourself. You're stronger than you know. I know you have a strong desire and a deep hunger for more: knowing you were made for more and better than your current situation.

Do you really want to be or do better? Do you want to be stronger? Do you want to live longer and have a better lifestyle? Well, then you have to do what it takes to make it happen. It's not going to just come to you, you have to get up and make it happen. The couch is always hiring and has plenty of openings available.

Are you ready to give up? Are you impressed by what you see? If not, then the only thing to do is make the required adjustments until you do. Get up! Get moving!

When can you stop? When will it be over? When will it get easier? You'll have to keep it up until you die. Fight for your life. Get up and get moving

Time isn't going to pause and wait for you. Life isn't a game that you can set on easy mode. Anything you want bad enough you have to be willing to fight for. Keep fighting, keep grinding, keep going. This is an all out war.

To accomplish your goals you must have laser focus upon whatever you want and go get it.

Easy is easy, but is that what's best for you? Be thankful that change isn't easy. It's the hardship, the consistency and work that makes you better and stronger. Push yourself past the old limitations of your existence and become more. Tear down the barriers of your old mindset and believe in yourself. You can do it, **FAILURE IS NOT AN OPTION.**

The End or The Beginning—Your Choice

Now that you've read Faith over Failure, my hope is that your faith in your personal success has increased. However, the work is just beginning.

In as great of detail as possible, describe your dream life.

Vision:
What it looks like?

What does your life's vision look like?

What does success look like to you?

What do you want/need to accomplish?

When will it be accomplished (Timeframe)?

Why:
Why do you want it?

Why is this so important to you?

Who will be positively impacted by your success?

What do you need to complete this?

Mission:
How will you make it happen?

What steps will you take to make this happen?

What are your goals for making this happen?

Who can you align with to help bring your vision to pass?

What is your main opposition to accomplishment?

What is your personal vision statement?

Vision Statement is a long term description of your life objective, most often for a ten year or longer time frame.

What is your personal mission statement?

The road map for how you will achieve the set goal in your vision statement. This helps to define, and clarify your purpose.

 Tip: You should consider doing this activity annually, monthly and even daily, to maximize your life's activities. The clearer you can make the image of your destiny, the easier it becomes to arrive at.

www.ingramcontent.com/pod-product-compliance
Lightning Source LLC
Chambersburg PA
CBHW060521130626

46553CB00002B/598